To Dad

Thanks for the campfires and constellations

Table of Contents

Nativity of Christ, Kefermarkt church, Austria

The Oak of Mamre

The Oak of Mamre, also called Abraham's Oak, is one
of the oak trees in Hebron, Israel, where Abraham
camped, Genesis 13, 18; Genesis 14, 13; Genesis 18, 1,
and built an altar. Genesis 13, 18. It was at these oak
trees that Abraham rested at the door of his tent in
the heat of the day when the three visitors came and
told him that within a year Sarah would bear his son.
Sarah laughed, prompting one of the visitors to ask if
anything was too great for the Lord. Sarah gave birth
and they named the son Isaac, a name which means
"he laughs." Genesis 18, 1-15; Genesis 21, 1-7.

From Dust to Stars

God said to Abraham, "Look and see
The dust upon the earth
For so shall your descendants be.
In you shall nations have their birth."

Later God said, "Look now and see
The stars up in the sky
For no more as dust shall your descendants be,
But as the stars on high."

Stars that for a time
Walk upon the earth
And in the darkness shine
To show man his own worth

And illumine the wonderous mystery
Of what men really are
Made in the very image of He
Who makes the shining star

The Cave of the Patriarchs

When Abraham's wife Sarah died, Abraham bought
the cave of Machpelah and the field of Ephron,
located east of the Oaks of Mamre in Hebron, Israel,
to bury Sarah. Genesis 23, 1-20. Abraham was also
buried at Machpelah, Genesis 25, 7-11, as were Isaac
and Rebekah, Genesis 49, 28-33 (see also Genesis 35,
27-29), and Jacob and Leah, Genesis 49, 28-33. In the
first century B.C. King Herod built the massive tomb
which still stands over the cave.

Joseph's Tomb

This is a photograph from the early 1900's showing Joseph's Tomb near Shechem in Israel where his bones were buried after being brought up out of Egypt. Joshua 24, 32.

When Joseph Came to the Land of Pharaoh

When Joseph came to the land of Pharaoh
Wearing chains, who could know?
The future lay in his hands
For all the Promised Land

When Moses fled the land of Pharaoh
Nearly dead, who could know?
The future lay in his hands
For all the Promised Land

Jesus Christ crucified
Blood and water flowing from His side
Who could know the Promised Land
Lay in His two pierced hands

This photograph from 2014 shows Joseph's Tomb
before it was attacked and burned in 2015.

Send Us Moses

Send us Moses to set us free
Send us Moses to part the sea
Pharaoh's coming and we've nowhere to flee
Send us Moses to set us free

We're sore oppressed through the day
Send us a Moses we pray
We're sore oppressed through the night
Save us like the Israelites

Men twist words like a knife
To take your freedom and take your life
To ruin names and plunder gold
But only God will judge your soul

Send us Moses to set us free
Send us Moses to part the sea
When Pharaoh comes and there's nowhere to flee
Send us Moses to set us free

The Burning Bush

The burning bush of Mount Sinai, where God spoke to Moses, Exodus 3 & 4, is still alive, located in St. Catherine's Monastery at Mt. Sinai, Egypt.

St. Catherine's Monastery, Egypt

Shiphrah and Puah

Pharaoh in his palace halls
Adorned in silk and porphyry
Gave order to his generals,
"Bring the midwives unto me."

"Those whose hands and hearts
Help mothers giving birth,
And with their sacred arts
Bring new life unto the earth."

"For the tribe of Abraham
Ever stronger grows,
And multiplies to fill this land
Where the Nile flows."

"This land that is mine,
This land that I command,
By Joseph's deep design
Now trembles before Abraham."

"Nor has bondage broken them
Or checked their growing might,
So let us strike the heart of Shem
With deeds as dark as night."

"By their very weakest ones
We shall bring about their doom
Let us strike their infant sons:
Their babes we shall consume."

So were the midwives brought
In their weakness before the king
In his tangling web caught
That they should do this thing

Within the palace walls
Past rows of polished pillars
Small within the royal halls
They were brought to be his killers

Shiphrah and Puah, they were named
And brought to tremble at the sight
Of Egypt in all its splendor famed
And Pharaoh in all his might

He said: "Shiphrah and Puah, hear
The voice of Pharaoh speak,
He who all men fear,
The mighty and the meek."

Then the dread command comes
From Pharaoh on his throne:
"Kill the Hebrew's baby sons
Upon the birthing stone."

"None need ever know
The deeds that you do
But Egypt will surely show
Its gratitude to you."

"For when their sons are gone
Their wealth shall pass to us.
They are weak, we are strong.
The world goes as it must."

Shiphrah and Puah knew
It was death to disobey
But this they could not do:
Infant children slay!

Though Pharaoh arrayed in royal hue
In Egypt may now hold sway
It was only as a steward who
Must give account one day

The hands that crook and flail now hold
Must one day pass into the grave
Where neither sharp of sword nor glint of gold
Had power to redeem or save

When would come that day
Was beyond Pharaoh's power to rule
But then must he account and pay
For deeds, kind or cruel

And as it was with Pharaoh
So was it with them, too
They must reap as they would sow
Shiphrah and Puah knew

So they left the palace walls
Passing rows of polished pillars
Though they may be small within his halls
They would not be Pharaoh's killers

And when the Hebrew mothers cried
"Shiphrah! Puah! Come!"
They helped bring forth the life inside
And gave to them their sons

And the Hebrews grew ever more
Life bloomed in Goshen's land
As Sarah's laughing daughters bore
Strong sons of Abraham

Pharaoh saw and gnashed his teeth
"Bring Shiphrah and Puah to me."
He held his sword within its sheath
And asked: "Whence come these children that I see?"

"For death was my wish,
From which no one could hide."
And so like Caiaphas
Unknowing he prophesied

They said, "The Hebrew women are strong,
Not like the daughters of the Nile.
They do not tarry long
In bringing forth their child."

"There is nothing we can do,
Before we even come
Their labor pains are through
And they hold their new born sons."

Pharaoh's hand fell from his hilt
He let the women go
But in his wish was guilt
And a seed of judgement sowed

While Shiphrah and Puah by their deeds
Saved a generation
And in time came from those seeds
A blessing for every nation

For they sowed the seeds of life
And for it were richly blessed
Each became a wife
With their own babies at their breast

Tree of Jesse, Beauvais Cathedral, France

Jonah and the Whale

Gather round the fire
And listen to my tale
I'll tell you of the story
Of Jonah and the whale

God told Jonah, "Now
To Nineveh you go.
To warn them of destruction
And the sorrow that they sow."

"For shall I not have pity
On the wayward sons of men
Who turn from Me and yet may still
Turn to Me again."

But Jonah told God, "No,
I'll turn my face from you.
I will not go to Nineveh
I'll sail the ocean blue."

Jonah ran from God
To Tarshish he was bound
When the waves came crashing
And the storm came whirling round

He was cast into the deep
Into the briny foam
In the belly of a whale
In darkness all alone

Beneath the surging flood
From the heart of the raging sea
He cried at last to God above,
"Lord, do not forsake me!"

God heard the voice that cried
He had pity on the man
And told the whale to cast him
Again onto dry land

"For," God said, "shall I not have pity
On the wayward sons of men
Who turn from me and yet may still
Turn to me again."

Jonah thanked the Lord
For the gift of His forgiving
For the chance to rise once more
And walk among the living

And Jonah walked the road
The Lord had marked for him
All the way to Nineveh
And they turned back again

The Lord is rich in mercy
To the wayward sons of men
Who turn away from Him and yet
Can turn to Him again

The Tomb of Jonah

This is the Tomb of Jonah, located in Mosul, Iraq, as it appeared before being blasted in 2014 by Islamic militants.

Clonfert Cathedral

Saint Brendan is buried at Clonfert Cathedral, located in County Galway, Ireland. He founded the monastery and church at Clonfert in 560 AD and it was here that he requested to be interred and was buried upon his death in 577.

Saint Brendan

At Saint Ailbe's Abbey
In the silent island of the sea
Saint Brendan asked to stay
But the ancient abbot answered, "Nay,"
"It is not to be," said he
"God calls you out to sea.
He has wonders there to show,
Wonders He wills that you would know.
He bids you journey, sails unfurled
Again into His wonder world
To search the secrets of His creation,
Secrets hid from time's foundation,
To see what yet no eye has seen,
And know what yet no man has dreamed."
And so upon the waves once more
Brendan pushed his coracle from the shore
And cast himself upon the brine
There to seek what he would find
Crossing wide the heaving swell
In search of what the world would tell
He set off to wander and explore
And knock upon the hidden door
And when he saw but could not see
What some hidden thing might be
He prayed to God fervently,
"Reveal to me this mystery,
Of Your world that You have made,

Let me know what is," he prayed
And as he sought so was it shown
And the secret of wonders to him made known
Thus many marvels did he find
Dazzling to man's questing mind
So that the hermit Paul confessed,
"Wandering Brendan, you are blessed
For to you has God revealed
Things which were before kept sealed."

So to all you who would seek to know
Who in dreams the seeds of wonder sow
Nurture the wonder so that it grows
And follow the way that Brendan shows
For since first there was mystery to unwind
It has been given to those who seek that they shall
find

Monhegan Island, Maine

A tradition says that Saint Brendan landed on
Monhegan Island, Maine. Ancient runes on adjacent
Manana Island are of possible Phoenician origin.

Saint Joan of Arc Chapel, Milwaukee, WI

The oldest church in America, the Saint Joan of Arc chapel was built in France beginning in the early 1400's, before Christopher Columbus was born. Saint Joan of Arc stopped in this chapel and prayed on her way to battle. The chapel also includes the Joan of Arc Stone. A statue of the Blessed Virgin Mary rested on the stone, and Saint Joan of Arc prayed to Mary for victory standing before the stone and statue, then kissed the stone on completing her prayers. At Saint Joan of Arc's kiss, the stone was transformed and to this day is cool to the touch and cooler than the stones around it. The chapel was disassembled stone by stone in France and transported to America, where it was erected first on Long Island, and later moved to its current home at Marquette University.

Saint Joan of Arc Chapel, Milwaukee, Wisconsin

In this chapel of her land
Saint Joan of Arc once prayed
To this stone reach out your hand
Feel the prayer she made

When darkness fell upon her land
Here she came to pray
And with Michael make her stand
On the warrior's way

Saint Joan prayed to The Virgin blessed
Whose statue stood upon this stone
Then to this stone her lips she pressed
A prayer in flesh and bone

This stone of prayer that she kissed
Since has born the mark
Through the ages' trackless mist
Of Saint Joan of Arc

Now her praying stone has come
To this land in need
Calling like a beating drum
Listen and give heed

The Last Words of Saint Joan of Arc

Bound upon the stake
Saint Joan of Arc had one request to make:
Lift the cross higher
That I may see before my eyes
Above the climbing fire
The love that never dies.

Saint Joan of Arc sculpture, Paris

Prayer to Saint Thomas Aquinas

Saint Thomas Aquinas
On my knees I pray
That ever you remind us
Truth is the only way

Saint Thomas Aquinas, from the Alter of the Dominican Church of St. Nicholas, Friesach, Austria

Tomb of Saint Thomas Aquinas, Toulouse, France

The Cathedral Church of Our Lady of Sorrows, Wrexham, Wales, which contains relics of Saint Richard Gwyn

Saint Richard Gwyn was born in Wales in 1537 and martyred at Wrexham in 1584. He attended Oxford and Cambridge, but was unable to graduate due to his Catholic faith and had to flee to the continent. He returned to Wales, married, had six children, and started a school. He was known for his humor, rhymes and songs. Sixteen years after his return, he was arrested and pressured to conform to the Church of England. At first he attempted to, out of fear for his wife and children, but he became physically ill attempting to attend one Anglican service, and was attacked by a swarm of hundreds of birds that almost killed him when he attempted to attend another. Whereupon he resolved to adhere to the Catholic faith. Then followed years as an outlaw, living on the run, moving his family from place to place. He was captured and imprisoned, escaped, and captured again. He then underwent four years of torture, ending in his martyrdom. Despite the years of torture, and promises of clemency if he would conform, Gwyn held fast to his faith. When at last they led him away for execution, he used the chains binding him as a rosary to pray. He was killed by being hung, cut down while still alive, disemboweled and having his still beating heart ripped from his chest, all while he yet lived.

Many miracles attended his sufferings. When a court officer attempted to read out false charges manufactured against Gwyn, the court officer was struck blind. The authorities took pains to hide this occurrence lest news of the miracle get out. Another: at the moment he was bound to the hurdle which dragged him to execution, rain began pelting hard. On the scaffold Gwyn observed, "God is merciful unto us; behold, the elements shed tears for our sins." Then, at the moment he died, the rain suddenly stopped.

Saint Richard Gwyn

Saint Richard Gwyn
I can hear your song on the wind
Sing your melody loud
From the midst of that shining cloud

The birds brought Elijah bread
To save his life, he was fed
The birds came to save you, too
And help you stand for what is true

He only wanted a quiet life
To raise his kids and love his wife
But the powers of the world could not stand
The conscience of a quiet man

So he was killed
Because he would not bow as they willed
In chains they led him away
Chains he used as a rosary to pray

Saint Richard Gwyn
Help me pray as you did then
Strengthen my failing hand
That I might join that heavenly band

Walsingham Priory Ruins

In 1061, near the small hamlet of Walsingham, England, the land known as "Mary's Dowry," The Blessed Virgin appeared to the lady Richeldis de Faverches and asked her to build a replica of the house in Nazareth where the angel Gabriel came to Mary with the Annunciation. Angels helped construct the house, and for half a millennium, beginning before William the Conqueror landed at Pevensey, Walsingham was one of Christendom's great pilgrimage destinations. But in 1534 Henry VIII declared himself head of the Church in England, and in 1538 government forces under the leadership of

Cromwell sacked and destroyed Walsingham. The Franciscan Order of Friar's Minor Conventual, known as the Grey Friars, also had an abbey at Walsingham, which was likewise sacked and destroyed. Yet pilgrimage to Walsingham continued over the centuries, even if clandestinely, and in recent times Walsingham has again become a major center of pilgrimage. Still, from its destruction by Cromwell no mass was said at the Grey Friar's abbey until finally in 2017 a Grey Friar priest returned and at last mass again was heard in the ruins of Walsingham Priory.

Our Lady of Walsingham, Slipper Chapel

The Slipper Chapel, Walsingham

The Slipper Chapel escaped destruction by Henry VIII and Cromwell. It is located one mile from where The Holy House had stood before it was burned to the ground. Pilgrims to The Holy House would take off their shoes in The Slipper Chapel and walk the final mile, The Holy Mile, barefoot. The chapel is dedicated to St. Catherine of Alexandria, the patron saint of pilgrims. On her feast day, November 25, the sun rises directly behind the altar. A chapel dedicated to St. Catherine of Alexandria is also located one mile outside of Nazareth in The Holy Land.

On the Occasion of Mass in the Ruins of Walsingham Priory, 2017

Grey Friar come under the sun
And lift your hands at Walsingham

Amid stones laid where friars prayed
The Holy Sacrifice was made

No roof or walls but still there calls
An echo from friars' choir stalls

From ages past and yet to come
At Walsingham

*The Franciscan Friary of the Grey Friars,
St. Mary's Priory, Walsingham*

Church of Domine Quo Vadis

According to tradition, during the persecutions of Nero Peter fled Rome to avoid crucifixion. At the junction of the Via Ardeatine and the Appian Way Christ appeared to Peter, walking toward Rome as Peter was walking away. Peter asked Him, "Lord, where are you going?" In Latin: "Domine, quo vadis?" Jesus answered that he was going to Rome to be crucified again since Peter would not. Peter then turned back to Rome to face his own crucifixion, fulfilling the words of Christ at the Sea of Galilee when He said: "'Amen, amen, I say to you, when you were younger, you used to dress yourself and go where you wanted; but when you grow old, you will stretch out your hands, and someone else will dress you and lead you where you do not want to go.' He said this signifying by what kind of death he would glorify God. And when He had said this, He said to him, "Follow me." John, 21, 18-19. Christ vanished from Peter's sight, though tradition says He left behind His own footprints imprinted in the marble paving stone on which He had stood. The church of Domine Quo Vadis, officially named The Church of Saint Mary in Palmis, stands at the place where Christ met Peter. Christs footprints in marble are still preserved in the church.

Footprints said to be those of Christ preserved in the Church of Domine Quo Vadis.

Quo Vadis

On the shores of Galilee
Jesus asked, "Do you love Me?"
The fisherman come from the sea,
Who shed his tears so bitterly,
Peter answered true,
"Yes, Lord, I love You."

On the shores of Galilee
Jesus asked, "Do you love Me?"
Peter said, "All things You know
Even to my very soul."
Peter answered true,
"Yes, Lord, I love You."

On the shores of Galilee
Jesus asked, "Do you love Me?"
Quo vadis he would ask one day,
And take his cross all the way.
Peter answered true,
"Yes, Lord, I love You."

Saint Thomas More and His Family

Sketch by Hans Holbein the Younger of Saint Thomas More (February 7, 1477-July 6, 1535) and his family. Saint Thomas More is in the center of the picture.

Saint Thomas More was known for being merry and brilliant. He was fluent in Latin, Greek, and French, played flute and viol, wrote prose (including the famous *Utopia*) and poetry, was a lawyer, ambassador, member of parliament and Lord Chancellor of England. He was eventually persecuted, imprisoned, and ultimately executed, because he would not renounce his Catholic faith. He died a martyr at Tower Hill by beheading, and his head was hung from London Bridge.

Prayer to Saint Thomas More

Pray for me now, O great Saint Thomas More
As the winds of storm howl round my door
Though all the world seem swept away
Help me be true to God, I pray

Night falls with a howl in the dark
Then come the ones bearing the mark
Stars fall and the sun shines no more
The blow falls, the howl is at my door

Help me fight with all my might
Against the howling of the night
For what a fool he would be
To trade away eternity

One day the world will be new
And the righteous rise that once they slew
All shall reap as they sow
And the crown of glory He will bestow

When the Skies are Dark

When the skies are dark
He makes the stars to shine
When the jars are empty
He turns water into wine

When there's no way forward
He makes the waters part
When the blow is too great
He binds the broken heart

So when the darkness finds you
And the sun won't shine
Remember God has told us
Forever you are mine

And if you find you've fallen
Reach out and take His hand
Ever He will hold you
And raise you up to stand

The Wedding Church at Cana

The Wedding Church at Cana is built over the site
where Jesus changed water into wine. John 2, 1-12.

Saint Bees Dragon Stone

The Saint Bees Dragon Stone is an ancient stone located in St. Bees Village on the coast of England. The village is named after St. Bees, also known as St. Brega, who tradition says was an Irish princess that arrived from across the sea in 850 and lived a life of great piety here. A church was founded, and later, around 1120, a Benedictine priory, which was suppressed by Henry VIII in 1539. The ruins of the priory continued to be used to various degrees until the mid-1800's when it was restored for use as a parish church.

The Ones Who Went Before

Past vales deep and mountains steep
Where wild rivers run
Where secrets keep and dragons sleep
Hidden from the sun

There tall stones stand upon the land
Raised in days of yore
A lasting brand and mark for man
From the ones who went before

The ones who made the shining blade
And learned the ancient lore
Who dragons slayed and darkness stayed
By battles won in war

When first there came the dragon bane
With fire in the night
On wing and flame to kill and maim
Men hid themselves in fright

And the dragons savage raved and ravaged
Over the naked land
To crush and kill as they willed
An evil none dared withstand

Then the dark that gnaws at men and laws
Allowed the beasts to reign
And their rending claws and scaly jaws
Ran red with the blood of the slain

From swirling skies, dark as lies
Shadows of dragon wings
Cast a haze that drove as slaves
Those God made as kings!

Yet in the dark was struck the spark
Of courage that flamed and grew
Like the break of dawn that riding on
Lights the world anew

Until no more to hide or turn aside
And hope the cup would pass
Nor avert their eyes as others died
Men stood to fight at last

From the valor born the blade took form
In the heat of glowing coals
Hammered and formed in the heart of storm
To flash like shining souls

Facing dangers dire from fang and fire
They fought through pain and fear
To win safe sleep in cottage and keep
For those that they held dear

They made seas sing and valleys ring
With the song of clashing steel
And fought to bring the blade's sting
Across the world on wheel and keel

Hunting the beasts they never ceased
Until the dragons were driven down
And the ancient dread was dead or fled
Into hiding under ground

With victory won the sword was hung
In its place upon the wall
And each bowed his head to honor the dead
Now gathered in heaven's hall

Then the stones were raised to mark the days
In remembrance evermore
Of the darkness slayed and the price once paid
By the ones who went before

But the sands of time swirl and blind
And weather the graying stone
Till worn away like a passing day
More is lost than known

And tales once told in hall and hold
In time are told no more
Like shadows in shade, memories fade
Of the ones who went before

Salt seas sigh and roll and rise
Washing on the shore
And whispered lies drown the battle cries
Of the ones who went before

Cold winds blow and shadows grow
Over things men know no more
And dark things stalk where once there walked
The ones who went before

The bright day ends and dusk descends
A howling is heard on the height
And stirring again deep in their dens
The dragons await the night

In nightmare dreams of terror screams
Where fire and fang devour
They taste again of the blood of men
And await their coming hour

To break like storm in a raging swarm
Upon the earth once more!
Come that day may all men pray
For the courage that went before

The Somerville Stone, Linton Church, Linton, Scotland

In the 12th Century a dragon lived at Linton Hill in Linton, Scotland. The dragon laid great waste to all the surrounding land until it was slain by John de Somerville. As reward for slaying the dragon, John de Somerville was knighted and made a baron.

On a Far and Distant Shore

On a far and distant shore
In a lost and lonely land
High upon a tor
Stood alone one man

The wind was cold and fierce
The sky was dark and gray
One star shone out to pierce
The twilight end of day

He held his sword on high
To catch its shining light
And cried unto the sky
"Dragon! Your end has come tonight!"

"For all the fallen ones
You've sent into the grave
The daughters and the sons
Fathers fought to save,"

"I've hunted you from land to land
Across this world that turns
Ever with this sword in hand
That for you ever yearns."

"There is no further place to fly,
You've nowhere left to run.
At this edge of sea and sky
At last shall it be done."

Deeper grew the dark
Descending into night
His sword shown like a spark
Of star fire burning bright

You chase only the wind,
Came the whispered, rasping reply
Go back, go back again.
Offered the soft, seductive lie

The voice rattled dry
As sand scoured bones
And thin as winds that sigh
Over the broken edge of stones

There is nothing here
But a phantom of your mind.
Your own ignorance and fear
Are all that you will find.

Look upon this land of mist,
In the midst of desert sea,
There is nothing more than this,
Nor could there ever be.

Only what your mind can grasp,
Only what your eye can see,
Only what your hand can clasp,
Only this will ever be.

So the voice hissed
Creeping into his mind
Like a cold and seeping mist
A choking, tangling vine

The words formed and broke
Like the shifting of the wind
Like a haze of drifting smoke
There, and gone again

Scattering like leaves that fall
Dissolving in the sounds of sea
Was it a voice at all?
Or only echoes of memory?

"Liar! Twister of words and meaning!"
He held his sword on high
"Plotter of ceaseless scheming!
Here is recompense for your lie!"

"Tell me the weight and measure
Of the ringing bell's chime,
Or keep if you can like treasure
Moments of passing time."

"What span has man's memory
That bridges age to age?
Where does the eye see
The idea on the written page?"

"Who can grasp the power
That a heart of hope will give,
Or fathom Love's darkest hour
Offered that man might live."

It hissed, *You cannot win,*
You shall surely die.
The man in answer grinned
"Come and prove it!" was his reply

Would you risk the wager
For those you've never known?
What profits you the danger
Of dying here alone?

"And now comes talk of dying
From one already dead.
Mine is life and trying
And a future yet ahead."

"For no matter what shall happen here
Your tale's already done,
While beyond this veil of tears
Mine is just begun."

"The choice put to me
Is between the dust and stars.
Offered me is eternity,
No greater gains there are."

"The only question when all is done
Is will I answer to His call?
If I do then I have won
And He shall raise me should I fall."

"Nor alone am I,
All around see how they shine,
More than the stars that fill the sky,
Witnesses of our destiny divine."

Then fell the foe
Unable more to fly
Dark coils of dread and woe
Fallen from the sky

A war cry split the night
As the man rushed upon the foe
Blade shining with the light
Of star fire's heaven glow

And so the blade went slashing
Amid fang and fire flashing
And the writhing tail's lashing
And his blows struck like thunder crashing!

Until the blade at last drove home
To rend the beast apart
Through scale and blood and bone
Into the blackened heart

The shrieking cry, the steaming hiss
The wracking of twisted form
The last vapors venomous
Then the calm after the storm

He pushed his coracle into the sea
The vast ocean once more to roam
The heavens above his guide to be
And followed the stars to home

The Bullion Stone
Found in Angus, Scotland, now located in the
Museum of Scotland in Edinburgh

Saint Michael Come to Me

Saint Michael come to me
Angel of God Almighty
With your sword burning bright
Scatter darkness with the light

On his rock above the sea
Michael helped set Erin free
When Patrick prayed to the Lord
God sent Michael with his sword

Off the coast of Cornwall
Were fishermen caught in a squall
Their lives Michael came to save
From the rocks beneath the waves

The Guardian of Israel
Revealer of Cacaxtla's well
At Bar Convent when the sisters prayed
Michael came to their aid

Saint Michael with his battle cry
Cast the enemy from heaven high
Crying out, "Who is like unto God?"
"Who is like unto God?"

Saint Michael's Mount, Cornwall

In 495 Saint Michael appeared on the rocks of Saint Michael's Mount in Cornwall, England, to save fisherman caught in a storm. Cornwall's Saint Michael's Mount is across the channel from Mont St. Michel, the famous island monastery of France where in 708 Saint Michael requested construction of a church in his honor. Like France's Mont St. Michel, at low tide a causeway connects Cornwall's Saint Michael's Mount to the mainland. The Benedictine monks of Mont St. Michel constructed the first church and monastery on Cornwall's Saint Michael's Mount in 1135. The Republic of France took France's Mont St. Michel in 1793, and the English crown took Cornwall's Saint Michael's Mount in 1548.

Bar Convent

Known as Bar Convent, the Convent of the Institute of the Blessed Virgin Mary located at Micklegate Bar, York, is a convent of nuns founded in 1686. The nuns faced great persecution, including imprisonment. In 1696 a mob attacked the convent and in fear the sisters prayed to Saint Michael for protection. Saint Michael appeared in the air above the convent riding on a white horse. The terrified mob fled and the sisters were saved.

Skellig Michael

According to tradition, Saint Michael appeared on Skellig Michael and assisted Saint Patrick in driving the serpents from Ireland. A monastic community was founded on Skellig Michael in the sixth century.

Cacaxtla, Mexico

During a smallpox epidemic in 1631, St. Michael appeared in Cacaxtla, Mexico and revealed a well whose waters miraculously cured the sick.

Simon of Cyrene

As I walk this road
No end to be seen
Help me bear my load
Simon of Cyrene

All the pain and dole
You saw when the wood was green
Help my aching soul
Simon of Cyrene

When you reached those pearly gates
And again you met the King
Were you glad you bore that weight,
Simon of Cyrene?

I wonder what the King will say
On that Judgement Day
To all the ones who help bear loads
On life's rocky roads

Detail from the Chapel of Simon of Cyrene on the Via
Dolorosa, Jerusalem

Saint Joseph with Jesus

Located at a former a Franciscan convent on the
Mount of Monks in Miranda de Ebro, Spain

Joseph Journeyed All the Way

Joseph journeyed all the way
To Bethlehem and Christmas Day
Beginning, as good things often do
In prayer to He Who makes things new
When Zechariah turned to God in prayer
To ask that God show him where
To find the man who should be
Wed to the Queen of Galilee
Wonder! An angel in answer came!
Saying, "Thus shall you know his name:
Every marriageable man call.
Have them bring their staffs all.
That Mary's husband should be found,
Place the staffs upon the ground
In the temple through the night
Then look again at morning light."
As the angel said so was it done
And the temple sealed at setting sun
And when they looked again at dawn's first hour
On Joseph's staff bloomed a pure white flower
And so Joseph was the one
Chosen by the Father for the Son
Thus was Joseph called to walk the way
With Mary, to Bethlehem and Christmas Day
To love and laugh and guard and guide

Every step at Mary's side
Walking with Mary all the way
To Bethlehem and Christmas Day

When Joseph learned of the child she carried
When they were but engaged and still unmarried
He thought that they must part their ways
And had he, what would have been of Christmas
Day?
But lo! An angel came in Joseph's dream
And told him of the coming King
And Joseph heard and obeyed
And his own part in salvation humbly played
That Salvation might be born
On that blessed Christmas morn

So went the three, mile upon dusty mile
Joseph, Mary and the Child
And at the manger Christmas morn
When came the time that Christ was born
There was Joseph at Mary's side
Ever vigilant for his bride
And the child born small and bare
Entrusted by God into his care
All through the night as cattle lowed
And the Christmas Star shining glowed
And shepherds came to behold
And three kings brought frankincense, myrrh and
gold
And in the sky they heard angels sing
And all creation bowed before its King

Joseph, dreamer of dreams
Guardian of the King
Who walked with Mary all the way
To Bethlehem and Christmas Day
Lead us also, we humbly pray
To the manger on Christmas Day

Window in Norwich Cathedral, England, showing
Joseph's Dream, The Circumcision, and The
Annunciation

The Royal Christmas Hall

Enter in the royal hall
Of the Christmas Queen
A lowly stable stall
Where is born the King

Manger wood for a thrown
Laid upon the straw
He whose coming for the prophets shown
Like a far off star they saw

Moses wrote how in the Garden
Was torn the ancient rift
When first a heart began to harden
And tried to steal the gift

Even then God promised One
Who would end their long exile
Born of the woman would be a Son
Who would all things reconcile

The ram crowned in thorn
On Mount Moriah died
For Abraham's son, his only born
In a sign of the Lamb God would provide

To David it was told
That his royal line
Would dominion ever hold
In Him, a King divine

Daniel counted down the years
In Babylon forlorn
Until the time should appear
When at last He would be born

Isaiah told how He would come
To dwell upon the earth
When given us would be the Son
Of the Virgin birth

Collegiate Church of Sant-Vulfran, Abbeville, France

Isaiah also told the mystery
Too great to understand
How at His Nativity
Would be born both God and man

The prophecies of Micah said
Bethlehem would be the place
Where in the House of Bread
Men would see the God-Man's face

But in watching through all the ages past
Who could have ever seen
That in such a hall as this at last
Would come to us our King?

A 1520's window from Mariawald Abbey, Germany

But even when she could not see
Mary in faith believed
And said, "So let it be done unto me,"
And in her womb conceived

At last it was the time
The Star shown in the sky
Wise men saw the sign
And angels sang on high

Though it may seem a lowly place
Still it was made by Him
And blessed in time by the grace
Of His birth within

So enter in this royal hall
Of our Christmas Queen
For in this noble stable stall
Today is born our King

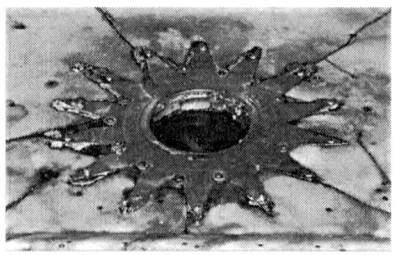

The exact spot where Jesus was born is marked by the
grotto star in the Church of the Nativity, built over
the cave of Jesus' nativity in Bethlehem.

Child of the Angel Dream

Child of the angel dream
Whom the prophets had in longing seen
Ancient King from of old
Bring frankincense, myrrh and gold
Where the manger wood His body holds
In Bethlehem as foretold
Laid in straw, yet angels sing!
At last, at last is come the King!
The Star above its message brings
And all the shining heavens ring
At last, at last is come our King!
No more shall darkness have its hold
Salvation comes as the prophets told
As Joseph had from the angel seen
Comes now the child of the angel dream
This, Eve's promised son
He is come! He is come! He is come!

Choir screen, Notre Dame Cathedral, France

Image Credits

8. *Joseph's Tomb from Mitzpe Yosef,* עדירל, [CC-BY-SA-4.0]
(https://commons.wikimedia.org/wiki/File:KeverYosef5600.JPG)

10. (Top Image, of the burning bush): *Bush of genista in place of the Burning Bush, Monastery of St Catherine, Sinai, Egypt*, Roland Unger, [CC-BY-SA-3.0,2.5,2.0,1.0]
(https://commons.wikimedia.org/wiki/File:StCatherineBush.jpg)

10. (Bottom image, of St. Catherine's Monastery): *Panoramic view of St Catherine's monastery, Sinai, Egypt*, Egghead06, [CC-Zero, Public Domain]
(https://commons.wikimedia.org/wiki/File:St_CatherinesPanorama.JPG)

16. *Tree of Jesse, pediment of the North gate of the Beauvais Cathedral*, Jastrow, [PD-self]
(https://commons.wikimedia.org/wiki/File:Tree_of_Jesse_Beauvais_cathedral_2007_06_17.jpg)

19. *Iraq (Babylonia). Nineveh, Tomb of Jonah*, Matson Collection, [PD-Matson, PD US no notice, Public Domain]
(https://commons.wikimedia.org/wiki/File:Iraq_(Babylonia)._Nineveh,_Tomb_of_Jonah_LOC_matpc.23039.jpg)

20. *Photograph of St Brendan's Cathedral, Clonfert, Co. Galway - detail of doorway*, JohnArmagh, [PD-

self, Public Domain]
(https://commons.wikimedia.org/wiki/File:Clonfert
Cathedral_Doorway.JPG)

22. *Monhegan Harbor, Monhegan Island, ME; from a 1909 postcard published by the Hugh C. Leighton Company, Portland, Maine*, Hugh C. Leighton Company, Portland, Maine, [PD US, Public Domain]
(https://commons.wikimedia.org/wiki/File:Monheg
an_Harbor,_Monhegan,_ME.jpg)

23. *Joan of Arc chapel. A church from the 15th century, initially built in France, moved to New York in 1927, and then to Milwaukee, Wisconsin, in 1964*, Leroy Skalstad, [CC-Zero, Public Domain]
(https://commons.wikimedia.org/wiki/File:Joan_of
_Arc_chapel-2290483.jpg)

25. *Equestrian statue of Joan of Arc by Emmanuel Frémiet (French, 1824–1910) at the Place des Pyramides, in Paris. Gilt bronze, 1899*, Jastrow, [PD-self, Public Domain]
(https://commons.wikimedia.org/wiki/File:Joan_of
_Arc_Emmanuel_Fremiet.jpg)

26. *Dominican-Order-church in Friesach: Main altar: Thomas Aquinas*, Neithan90, [CC-Zero, Public Domain]
(https://commons.wikimedia.org/wiki/File:Friesach
_-_Dominikanerkirche_-_Hochaltar_-
_Hl_Thomas_von_Aquin1.jpg)

27. *Tomb of St. Thomas Aquinas, in les Jacobins church, Toulouse*, KimonBerliln, [CC-BY-SA-2.0] (https://commons.wikimedia.org/wiki/File:Reliques _de_saint_Thomas_d%27Aquin_(3211538222).jpg)

28. *Wrexham RC Cathedral, Wales*, JohnArmagh, [PD-user, Public Domain] (https://commons.wikimedia.org/wiki/File:Wrexha mRCCathedral.JPG)

31. *Walsingham Abbey Remains*, David P Orman, [CC-BY-SA-3.0-migrated, CC-BY-2.5] (https://commons.wikimedia.org/wiki/File:Walsing hamAbbeyRemains.jpg)

32. *The statue of Our Lady of Walsingham, the Slipper Chapel, Walsingham, Norfolk, England*, Thorvaldsson, [CC-BY-3.0] (https://commons.wikimedia.org/wiki/File:Our_La dy_of_Walsingham_III.JPG)

33. *Slipper Chapel, Houghton St Giles, Norfolk*, John Salmon, [CC-BY-SA-2.0] (https://commons.wikimedia.org/wiki/File:Slipper_ Chapel,_Houghton_St_Giles,_Norfolk_- _geograph.org.uk_-_319689.jpg)

34. *Panoramic composite photograph of St Mary's Friary, Walsingham, Norfolk*, JohnArmagh, [CC-BY-SA-3.0] (https://commons.wikimedia.org/wiki/File:Walsing hamFriary.jpg)

35. *Eglise Domine Quo Vadis ou Santa Maria in Palmis de Rome dans le quartier de l'Appio Latino*, LPLT, [CC-BY-SA-3.0] (https://commons.wikimedia.org/wiki/File:Eglise_Domine_Quo_Vadis_de_Rome.JPG)

36. *Roma, via Appia Antica, Chiesa del Quo vadis: ex voto romano ritenuto l'impronta dei piedi di San Pietro*, Lalupa, [PD-user, Public Domain] (https://commons.wikimedia.org/wiki/File:I_piedi_del_quo_vadis.jpg)

38. *Study for the Family Portrait of Thomas More. Pen and brush in black on top of chalk sketch, 38.9 × 52.4 cm. Kupferstichkabinett, Öffentliche Kunstsammlung, Base*, Stephanie Buck, *Hans Holbein*, Cologne: Könemann, 1999, ISBN 3829025831, [CC-PD-Mark, PD-Art (PD-old-100), Public Domain] (https://commons.wikimedia.org/wiki/File:Study_for_portrait_of_the_More_family,_by_Hans_Holbein_the_Younger.jpg)

41. *Weddingchurch in Kafr Kanna*, Jayme del Rosario, [CC-BY-2.0] (https://commons.wikimedia.org/wiki/File:Catholic_Wedding_Church_of_Cana.jpg)

42. *Romanesque lintel showing St Michael fighting a dragon. Date Ca. 1120 (Zarnecki)*, Doug Sim, [CC-BY-SA-3.0]

47. *Mediaeval carving sometimes known as the
"Somervail Stone", currently situated above the
doorway of the church at Linton, Scottish Borders.
The scene shows a knight on horseback, clad in a
tunic or hauberk, with a round helmet, urging his
horse against two large animals, the foreparts of
which only are visible, and plunging his lance into the
throat of one. Behind him is supposed to be the
outline of another creature, apparently of a lamb. The
image is said by tradition to be connected to the story
of the Worm of Linton, although the heads of the
monsters in this image are more like those of
quadrupeds than of serpents*, Pasicles, [CC-Zero,
Public Domain]

53. *The Bullion slab, a Pictish image stone showing a
warrior drinking from a large horn (terminating in a
bird's head) while on horseback. Discovered in 1933
during road construction at Invergowrie, Scotland,
now kept in the Museum of Scotland in Edinburgh]
(ancient-scotland.co.uk). This image shows a small-
scale replica of the stone, which is longer and more
finely carved*, no author listed, [CC-PD-Mark, PD
Old, Public Domain]

(https://commons.wikimedia.org/wiki/File:Pictdrin
kinghorn.jpg)

55. *Saint Michael's Mount in Cornwall, United
Kingdom*, Author Unkown, [PD 1923, Public
Domain]
(https://commons.wikimedia.org/wiki/File:England
-Saint-Michaels-Mount-1900-1.jpg)

56. *York*, Tim Green from Bradford, [CC-BY-2.0]
(https://commons.wikimedia.org/wiki/File:Bar_Co
nvent_(11278851965).jpg)

57. *The Skellig Michael*, Jerzy Strzelecki, [CC-BY-SA-
3.0]
(https://commons.wikimedia.org/wiki/File:Skellig_
Michael03(js).jpg)

58. *Jerusalem, Via Dolorosa (corner with El Wad),
Station V*, Berthold Werner, [PD-self, Public Domain]

59. *Statue of Saint Joseph with Jesus, Hotel del
Convento, Miranda de Ebro, Spain*, Jebulon, [CC-
Zero, Public Domain]
(https://commons.wikimedia.org/wiki/File:Statue_S
aint_Joseph_Jésus_Miranda_de_Ebro.jpg)

62. *Joseph's dream, The Circumcision, and The
Annunciation. Glass by Hardman, 1868. Pic by Jenny*,
Jenny & Jenny from Lincoln, UK, [CC-BY-2.0]
(https://commons.wikimedia.org/wiki/File:Norwic

h_Cathedral,_Jesus_chapel_window_(24204588706).jpg)

64. *The Nativity altar, Collégiale Saint-Vulfran, Abbeville, Somme, France*, Mattana, [CC-BY-2.0] (https://commons.wikimedia.org/wiki/File:Abbeville,_Église_Saint-Vulfran_23.JPG)

65. *Stained glass from Mariawald Abbey depicting the Nativity*, Everhard Rensig or Gerhard Remisch, PD-Art (PD-US), Public Domain] (https://commons.wikimedia.org/wiki/File:Nativity-Mariawald-Abbey.jpg)

66. *The birthplace of Jesus in the Grotto of the Nativity*, Mark87 at English Wikipedia, [PD-user, Public Domain] (https://commons.wikimedia.org/wiki/File:Nativity_Grotto_Star.jpg)

67. *Choir screen at cathedral Notre-Dame de Paris, France. Detail of the north side: Mary visits Elizabeth, Annunciation to the Shepherds, Nativity of Christ, Adoration of the Magi*, Uoaei1, [CC-BY-SA-4.0] (https://commons.wikimedia.org/wiki/File:Paris_Notre-Dame_Choir_Screen_North_01.JPG)

About the Author

Jake Frost is the author of two other books: <u>Catholic Dad, (Mostly) Funny Stories of Faith, Family, and</u>

<u>Fatherhood</u>, and <u>The Happy Jar</u>, a children's picture book he wrote and illustrated.

Printed in Poland
by Amazon Fulfillment
Poland Sp. z o.o., Wrocław